Table of Contents

Introduction

Chapter 1. The History of the German legal system. Where did it begin?

Chapter 2. The influence of Roman Law on German Law.

Chapter 3. The development of German law during and after Napoleon.

Chapter 4. The German legal system during Nazi Germany.

Chapter 5. The interaction between different branches of Government in Germany.

Chapter 6. The role of the judiciary in Germany.

Chapter 7. The head of the German Legal System.

Chapter 8. The structure of the German Courts.

Chapter 9. The influence of the German government on the German legal system.

Chapter 10. The working hours of the German Courts.

Chapter 11. German laws in Austria and in Switzerland.

Chapter 12. Places in the world where German Law has an impact.

Chapter 13. A Comparison between British Law and German Law.

Chapter 14. A comparison between American law and German Law.

Chapter 15. A Comparison between French Law and German Law.

Chapter 16. The reputation of the German Courts.

Chapter 17. Practicing lawyers in Germany.

Chapter 18. Important legal issues in Germany.

Chapter 19. The biggest challenges to German law in the future.

Chapter 20. Prominent law cases in Germany.

Chapter 21. The training of lawyers in Germany.

Chapter 22. The most broken laws in Germany.

Chapter 23. A list of some common German legal terms.

Chapter 24. How do you make a Vertrag (contract) in Germany?

Chapter 25. What is meant by Recht in German?

Chapter 26. Does everybody have a Recht?

Chapter 27. The balance between individual rights and freedoms and the interests of society.

Chapter 28. Do foreigners have more rights in Germany than native Germans?

Chapter 29. When do you have to go to the Gericht (court)?

Chapter 30. Is the Strafgesetzbuch based on the laws of Napoleon?

Chapter 31. The Strafgesetzbuch.

Chapter 32. The Bürgerliches Gesetzbuch.

Chapter 33. The Bürgerliches Gesetzbuch, a short history.

Chapter 34. Arbeitsrecht - Labour Law

Chapter 35. Urheberrecht - Copyright Law

Chapter 36. The German Markenrecht - Trademark Law

Chapter 37. Patentrecht - Patent Law

Chapter 38. Wettbewerbsrecht - Competition Law

Chapter 39. Verwaltungsrecht - Administrative Law

Chapter 40. Zivilprozessrecht - Civil Procedure Law

Chapter 41. Strafprozessrecht - Criminal Procedure Law

Chapter 42. Europäisches Recht - European Law

Chapter 43. The relationship between EU Law and German Law.

Conclusion

Introduction

German law is one of the most influential legal systems in the world, shaping not only the legal landscape of Germany, but also influencing the development of legal systems around the world. With its roots in Roman law and the development of the German Civil Code in the 19th century, German law is a complex and sophisticated system that governs a wide range of legal issues, from criminal law to contract law, and from public law to private law.

This book provides a comprehensive introduction to the German legal system, exploring its historical development, its fundamental principles, and its current state of evolution. Through a series of chapters, the book delves into the key components of the German legal system, including the role of the judiciary, the interaction between different branches of government, and the balance between individual rights and freedoms and the interests of society.

Whether you are a student of law, a practitioner, or simply someone with an interest in legal systems, this book provides a comprehensive and accessible introduction to the world of German law. With its clear and concise writing style, and its rich array of case studies, examples, and insights, this book will help you to understand the intricacies of the German legal system and appreciate its significance both within Germany and on the global stage.

Chapter 1. The History of the German legal system. Where did it begin?

The German legal system has its roots in Roman law and the common law systems. However, the modern German legal system can be traced back to the Napoleonic Code, which was introduced in 1804.

The Napoleonic Code, also known as the French Civil Code, was a comprehensive legal code that served as the basis for modern civil law systems in many countries, including Germany. The Code introduced a number of important concepts, such as the principle of equality before the law, the protection of property rights, and the separation of powers.

After the fall of Napoleon, the German states were reorganized and the German Confederation was established in 1815. The Confederation adopted a legal system based on the Napoleonic Code, which was known as the Bürgerliches Gesetzbuch (BGB) or the Civil Code. The BGB remains the core of the German legal system to this day.

In addition to the BGB, the German legal system also includes a number of other important laws, such as the Criminal Code (Strafgesetzbuch), the Commercial Code (Handelsgesetzbuch), and the Labor Law (Arbeitsrecht). These laws have been developed over time to reflect the changing needs and priorities of German society, and they continue to evolve to meet the changing demands of the 21st century.

Overall, the German legal system has a rich and complex history, reflecting the influences of both Roman law and common law, as well as the impact of historical events such as the Napoleonic era and the unification of Germany in the 19th century. Today, the German legal system is considered to be one of the most advanced and sophisticated in the world, and it continues to play a critical role in shaping the lives of Germans and in protecting the rights and interests of citizens.

Chapter 2. The influence of Roman Law on German Law.

Roman law has had a significant influence on German law. The German legal system, like many other European legal systems, has its roots in Roman law.

Roman law was a comprehensive legal system that was developed during the Roman Empire. It covered a wide range of legal issues, including property law, contract law, and criminal law. Roman law was based on the idea of the rule of law, and it was designed to provide a stable and consistent framework for the administration of justice.

After the fall of the Roman Empire, Roman law was continued in the form of the Corpus Iuris Civilis, which was a collection of legal texts that formed the basis of civil law in the Byzantine Empire. During the Middle Ages, Roman law was widely studied and used in Europe, and it became the basis of the civil law systems that developed in many countries, including Germany.

In Germany, Roman law was first introduced during the High Middle Ages, and it was used by the courts and legal scholars to develop a comprehensive legal system. During the 19th century, the influence of Roman law was further reinforced with the introduction of the Napoleonic Code, which was based on Roman law principles. Today, Roman law continues to play an important role in German law, and it is reflected in many areas of the German legal system, such as contract law and property law.

Overall, the influence of Roman law on German law has been profound, and it has helped to shape the development of the German legal system over many centuries. Roman law has contributed to the stability and consistency of German law, and it has played a critical role in ensuring that the German legal system provides a fair and effective framework for the administration of justice.

Chapter 3. The development of German law during and after Napoleon.

The development of German law during and after Napoleon was shaped by the impact of the Napoleonic Code and the political and social changes of the time.

The introduction of the Napoleonic Code in 1804 marked a turning point in the development of German law. The Code brought with it a number of important legal concepts, such as the principle of equality before the law, the protection of property rights, and the separation of powers. These concepts formed the basis of the Bürgerliches Gesetzbuch (BGB), or the Civil Code, which was introduced in the German states after the fall of Napoleon.

After the establishment of the German Confederation in 1815, the BGB was adopted as the core of the German legal system. The Civil Code provided a comprehensive framework for civil law in Germany, and it served as the basis for the development of other key areas of German law, such as the Criminal Code (Strafgesetzbuch) and the Commercial Code (Handelsgesetzbuch).

During and after the unification of Germany in the 19th century, German law continued to evolve and adapt to the changing needs of society. For example, the introduction of the Social Democratic Party in the late 19th century led to the development of labor law, which was designed to protect the rights and interests of workers. Similarly, the growth of commerce and industry during this period led to the development of commercial law, which helped to regulate and promote trade and commerce.

After the end of World War II, German law underwent a significant transformation, as the country was divided into two separate states, the Federal Republic of Germany (West Germany) and the German Democratic Republic (East Germany). During this time, the German legal system was influenced by different ideologies and political systems, with the West German legal system drawing on the principles of the BGB and the common law system, while the East German legal system was based on the Soviet legal system.

After the reunification of Germany in 1990, the German legal system underwent further changes, as the country integrated the legal systems of the former East and West Germany. Today, the German legal system is considered to be one of the most advanced and sophisticated in the world, and it continues to play a critical role in shaping the lives of Germans and in protecting the rights and interests of citizens.

Chapter 4. The German legal system during Nazi Germany.

During the Nazi era in Germany, from 1933 to 1945, the legal system was fundamentally altered. The Nazi regime stripped the German courts of their independence and the legal system was used to enforce the policies of the Nazi party.

One of the first steps taken by the Nazis was to purify the legal profession by removing Jews, political opponents, and other perceived enemies of the state. This led to the appointment of judges and lawyers who were sympathetic to the Nazi cause.

The Nazis also introduced a number of laws and regulations that were designed to control and suppress political opposition, such as the Enabling Act of 1933, which gave Hitler the power to make laws without the approval of the Reichstag. This act was used to pass a number of laws that stripped citizens of their civil rights and freedoms, and it was used to justify the arrest and persecution of political opponents.

The Nazi legal system also created a number of special courts and tribunals, such as the People's Court, which were used to prosecute political opponents and enemies of the state. These courts were notorious for their speed and lack of due process, and they often resulted in harsh punishments, including death sentences.

The Nazi regime also introduced a number of laws that were designed to discriminate against Jews and other minority groups. These laws were used to strip Jews of their rights and freedoms, and they were used to justify the arrest and persecution of Jews, Roma, homosexuals, and other groups.

Chapter 5. The interaction between different branches of Government in Germany.

In Germany, the different branches of government interact with each other to ensure that the country is governed in a democratic, efficient, and effective manner. The three main branches of government in Germany are the legislative branch, the executive branch, and the judicial branch.

Legislative Branch: The legislative branch of government in Germany is represented by the German Bundestag (federal parliament) and the Bundesrat (federal council). The Bundestag is the lower house of the German federal parliament and is responsible for passing laws and creating legislation. The Bundesrat, on the other hand, represents the 16 federal states and is responsible for representing the interests of the states in federal legislation.

Executive Branch: The executive branch of government in Germany is represented by the federal government, which is led by the Federal Chancellor. The Federal Chancellor is appointed by the President and is responsible for the administration of the country and the implementation of laws and policies.

Judicial Branch: The judicial branch of government in Germany is represented by the Federal Constitutional Court, the Federal Court of Justice, and the regional courts. The Federal Constitutional Court is responsible for interpreting the constitution and ensuring that laws are in compliance with the constitution, while the Federal Court of Justice is responsible for resolving disputes and interpreting laws. The regional courts are responsible for hearing criminal and civil cases and enforcing laws.

The different branches of government in Germany interact with each other through a system of checks and balances, with each branch having the power to limit the actions of the others. For example, the legislative branch can override executive decisions, while the judiciary can declare laws unconstitutional. This system of checks and balances ensures that power is distributed among the different branches of government, promoting accountability and preventing the abuse of power.

Chapter 6. The role of the judiciary in Germany.

The judiciary plays a critical role in the German legal system, serving as the impartial arbiter of disputes and protecting the rule of law. The judiciary is an independent branch of government, separate from the legislative and executive branches, and its role is to interpret and apply the law in a fair and impartial manner.

In Germany, the judiciary is responsible for resolving a wide range of disputes, including civil and criminal cases, commercial disputes, and administrative appeals. The judiciary also plays a critical role in interpreting and applying EU law and ensuring that it is in compliance with the German constitution.

The German judiciary is composed of several different types of courts, including the lower courts, the intermediate appellate courts, and the highest court, the Federal Constitutional Court. The lower courts are responsible for resolving disputes at the first instance, while the intermediate appellate courts are responsible for hearing appeals from the lower courts. The Federal Constitutional Court is the highest court in Germany and is responsible for interpreting the constitution, resolving disputes between the federal and state governments, and reviewing the constitutionality of legislation.

In addition to resolving disputes and interpreting the law, the judiciary also plays an important role in protecting individual rights and freedoms. The German constitution provides for the protection of fundamental rights, including the right to a fair trial, the right to privacy, and the right to freedom of expression, and the judiciary is responsible for ensuring that these rights are respected and upheld.

The judiciary plays a critical role in the German legal system, serving as the impartial arbiter of disputes, interpreting and applying the law, and protecting individual rights and freedoms. The independence of the judiciary, the impartiality of its decisions, and its commitment to the rule of law are key elements of the German legal system and ensure that justice is served efficiently and effectively.

Chapter 7. The head of the German Legal System.

The head of the German legal system is the Federal President of Germany. The Federal President acts as the head of state and represents the unity of the nation. He is responsible for ensuring the proper functioning of the legal system and for safeguarding the independence of the judiciary.

The Federal President is also responsible for appointing judges and prosecutors to the highest courts, and he plays a critical role in maintaining the independence of the German legal system. In addition, the Federal President can grant pardons and clemency, and he is responsible for signing laws into effect.

While the Federal President is the head of the German legal system, the administration of justice is the responsibility of the courts and the judiciary. The courts in Germany are divided into two main categories: the civil courts and the criminal courts. The civil courts are responsible for resolving disputes between private individuals, while the criminal courts are responsible for hearing criminal cases.

Overall, the German legal system is highly independent, impartial, and well-respected, and the head of the system, the Federal President, plays a critical role in ensuring the proper functioning of the legal system and safeguarding its independence.

Chapter 8. The structure of the German Courts.

The structure of the German courts is divided into two main branches: the civil and the criminal justice system. The civil justice system handles civil cases, such as disputes over contracts, property rights, and inheritance, while the criminal justice system handles criminal cases, such as theft, assault, and murder.

The German court system is divided into several levels, starting from the local courts and working up to the federal level. The local courts are the lowest level of the court system, and they handle cases involving minor offenses and civil disputes. There are also specialized courts, such as labor courts and administrative courts, that handle specific types of cases.

The intermediate level of the court system is the Regional Court (Landgericht), which handles more serious offenses and civil disputes. The Regional Court is the first level of appeal, and it has the power to hear appeals from decisions made by the local courts.

The highest level of the civil court system is the Federal Court of Justice (Bundesgerichtshof), which serves as the final court of appeal for civil cases. The Federal Court of Justice is the highest authority on civil law in Germany, and its decisions are binding on all lower courts.

In the criminal justice system, the intermediate level of the court system is the Regional Criminal Court (Kriminalgericht), which handles serious criminal cases. The Regional Criminal Court is the first level of appeal, and it has the power to hear appeals from decisions made by the local courts.

The highest level of the criminal court system is the Federal Court of Justice, which serves as the final court of appeal for criminal cases. The Federal Court of Justice is the highest authority on criminal law in Germany, and its decisions are binding on all lower courts.

Overall, the German court system is designed to provide a fair and effective framework for the administration of justice, and it is based on the principles of independence, impartiality, and the rule of law. The German courts play a critical role in protecting the rights and interests of citizens, and they ensure that the legal system provides a stable and consistent framework for resolving disputes.

Chapter 9. The influence of the German government on the German legal system.

The German government has a significant influence on the German legal system, although the German legal system is designed to be independent and impartial. The German Constitution, the Basic Law, provides a clear separation of powers between the legislative, executive, and judicial branches of government, and it enshrines the independence of the judiciary.

The German government is responsible for creating laws and regulations, and it has the power to pass legislation that affects the legal system. The government can also influence the legal system through the appointment of judges and prosecutors, as well as by funding and supporting the courts.

However, the independence of the judiciary is protected by the Basic Law, and the German courts have the power to review and strike down laws that are deemed unconstitutional. This ensures that the government does not have unlimited power to influence the legal system, and it helps to protect the rights and freedoms of citizens.

Overall, the German legal system is designed to be independent and impartial, and the government plays a significant role in shaping the legal system through its legislative power. However, the independence of the judiciary and the protection of individual rights are carefully guarded, and the government is limited in its ability to influence the legal system.

Chapter 10. The working hours of the German Courts.

The working hours of the German courts vary depending on the type of court and the jurisdiction in which it operates. In general, German courts are open during regular business hours, typically from Monday to Friday, from around 9:00 a.m. to 5:00 p.m.

However, the specific working hours of individual courts can vary, and some courts may have extended hours to accommodate individuals who are unable to attend during regular business hours. Some courts may also be open on weekends or evenings for specific purposes, such as hearings in urgent cases or for individuals who are unable to attend during regular business hours.

In addition to regular business hours, German courts may also be open for specific purposes, such as for the submission of documents or for the filing of appeals. The specific procedures for accessing the courts and filing documents may vary depending on the jurisdiction and the type of court.

Overall, the working times of German courts are designed to be accessible and convenient for individuals who need to use the courts to resolve legal disputes or to access justice. The German legal system is committed to ensuring that individuals are able to access the courts in a timely and convenient manner, and that justice is served efficiently and effectively.

Chapter 11. German laws in Austria and in Switzerland.

The legal systems of Austria and Switzerland are not based on German law but they have been strongly influenced by German law. While there are some similarities between the legal systems of these countries, they each have their own unique legal traditions and systems.

Austria has a civil law system that is influenced by the Napoleonic Code and the Austrian Civil Code.

Switzerland has a mixed legal system that combines elements of both civil law and common law. The Swiss legal system is influenced by Roman law, as well as the Napoleonic Code and German law.

While there may be some similarities between the legal systems of these countries and Germany, each country has its own laws, regulations, and legal procedures, and individuals should familiarize themselves with the specific legal requirements of the country in which they reside or do business.

Chapter 12. Places in the world where German Law has an impact.

German law has an impact in several countries, including:

Germany: German law is the primary legal system in Germany and applies to all citizens and residents.

Austria: Austrian law has been heavily influenced by German law and is based on the German Civil Code.

Belgium: German law has played a significant role in the development of Belgian civil law, particularly in the areas of commercial and economic law.

Switzerland: Swiss law has also been influenced by German law, particularly in the area of contract law.

Liechtenstein: The legal system of Liechtenstein is based on Swiss and German law, with the country being a member of the German-speaking community.

Additionally, German law has had an impact on the legal systems of other countries through the principles of comparative law and the influence of German legal thought on international law.

Chapter 13. A Comparison between British Law and German Law.

British law and German law are two distinct legal systems with some similarities and differences. Here are a few of the key comparisons:

Historical Development: The history of German law can be traced back to the Holy Roman Empire and the development of the German Civil Code in the 19th century, but it has roots in earlier legal systems such as Roman law and canon law. The historical development of British law, on the other hand, goes back to the early Middle Ages, with the Norman Conquest in 1066 being a significant turning point in the development of the English legal system. The development of the common law system in England and the expansion of the British Empire also played a significant role in the history of British law.

Legal System: British law is based on the common law system, where judicial precedents and custom play a significant role, while German law follows a civil law system, where laws are codified and legal principles are based on written laws.

Judiciary: The British judiciary is independent and operates separately from the other branches of government, while the German judiciary is subject to some degree of government influence and control.

Criminal Law: British criminal law is focused on the protection of individual rights and freedoms, while German criminal law places a greater emphasis on the protection of society and the welfare of the community.

Contract Law: British contract law is based on the principle of freedom of contract, while German contract law is more heavily regulated, with specific laws governing the formation, performance, and termination of contracts.

Public Law: German public law is more interventionist, with a strong focus on government regulation, while British public law places a greater emphasis on individual rights and freedoms.

Overall, while both legal systems share some similarities, they differ in their historical development, legal structures, and approach to various legal areas.

Chapter 14. A comparison between American law and German Law.

American law and German law are two distinct legal systems with some similarities and differences. Here are a few of the key comparisons:

Historical Development: American law has its roots in British common law and has been influenced by the principles of the Enlightenment, while German law has its roots in Roman law and the development of the German Civil Code in the 19th century.

Legal System: American law follows a common law system, where judicial precedents and custom play a significant role, while German law follows a civil law system, where laws are codified and legal principles are based on written laws.

Constitution: The American legal system is based on a written constitution, the U.S. Constitution, which outlines the structure and powers of government, while the German legal system is based on a Basic Law, which serves as a constitution and outlines the basic principles of German democracy.

Judiciary: The American judiciary is independent and operates separately from the other branches of government, while the German judiciary is subject to some degree of government influence and control.

Criminal Law: American criminal law places a strong emphasis on individual rights and freedoms, including the right to a fair trial and the protection against self-incrimination, while German criminal law places a greater emphasis on the protection of society and the welfare of the community.

Contract Law: American contract law is based on the principle of freedom of contract, while German contract law is more heavily regulated, with specific laws governing the formation, performance and termination of contracts.

Public Law: American public law places a strong emphasis on individual rights and freedoms, including the protection of property rights, while German public law is more interventionist, with a strong focus on government regulation.

Overall, while both legal systems share some similarities, they differ in their historical development, legal structures, and approach to various legal areas.

Chapter 15. A Comparison between French Law and German Law.

French law and German law are two distinct legal systems with some similarities and differences. Here are a few of the key comparisons:

Historical Development: French law has its roots in the Napoleonic code, which was developed during the French Revolution, while German law has its roots in Roman law and the development of the German Civil Code in the 19th century.

Legal System: French law follows a civil law system, where laws are codified and legal principles are based on written laws, while German law also follows a civil law system, where laws are codified and legal principles are based on written laws.

Judiciary: The French judiciary operates independently and is subject to limited government influence, while the German judiciary is subject to some degree of government influence and control.

Criminal Law: French criminal law places a strong emphasis on the protection of individual rights and freedoms, including the right to a fair trial, while German criminal law places a greater emphasis on the protection of society and the welfare of the community.

Contract Law: French contract law is heavily regulated, with specific laws governing the formation, performance and termination of contracts, while German contract law is also regulated, with specific laws governing the formation, performance and termination of contracts.

Public Law: French public law is interventionist, with a strong focus on government regulation, while German public law also places a strong emphasis on government regulation, but also takes into account individual rights and freedoms.

Overall, while both legal systems share some similarities, they differ in their historical development, legal structures, and approach to various legal areas.

Chapter 16. The reputation of the German Courts.

The German courts have a strong reputation for being independent, impartial, and well-respected. The German legal system is considered to be one of the most advanced and sophisticated in the world, and the German courts are known for their efficiency, fairness, and impartiality.

The German courts are highly respected for their expertise in the law, and they are seen as a trusted source of legal guidance. The independence of the German courts is guaranteed by the constitution, and they are free from political or outside influence. This independence ensures that the German courts are able to make impartial decisions that are based solely on the law and the facts of the case.

The German legal system is also known for its efficiency, and the German courts are known for their ability to quickly and effectively resolve legal disputes. The German courts are well-equipped to handle complex legal cases, and they are able to provide quick and effective resolutions to disputes. This efficiency is a result of the well-trained and experienced judges, the use of modern technology, and the well-established legal procedures that are in place.

The reputation of the German courts is also enhanced by their commitment to upholding the rule of law and protecting the rights and interests of citizens. The German courts take their responsibilities seriously, and they are committed to ensuring that the legal system provides a fair and effective framework for the administration of justice.

Overall, the reputation of the German courts is one of the strongest in the world, and they are highly respected for their independence, impartiality, expertise, and efficiency. The German courts play a critical role in maintaining the stability and fairness of the German legal system, and they are a key component of the German democratic system.

Chapter 17. Practicing lawyers in Germany.

In Germany, practicing lawyers, also known as "Rechtsanwälte," provide legal advice and representation to clients in a variety of legal matters. They may work in private law firms, government agencies, or other legal organizations, and they may specialize in areas such as criminal law, corporate law, or tax law.

To become a practicing lawyer in Germany, one must complete a university degree in law, pass the First and Second State Exams, complete a two-year legal clerkship, and be admitted to the bar.

Once admitted to the bar, a lawyer in Germany must comply with professional ethical standards and continuing education requirements. They must also maintain professional liability insurance, which protects clients against any losses that may result from their legal representation.

Practicing lawyers in Germany play a crucial role in ensuring that individuals and businesses receive effective legal representation and advice, and they help to uphold the rule of law and protect the rights of citizens.

Chapter 18. Important legal issues in Germany.

Data protection and privacy: Germany has some of the strictest data protection laws in the world, and privacy is a highly valued right in the country. The country's Federal Data Protection Act and the EU's General Data Protection Regulation (GDPR) are among the key legal instruments that govern data protection and privacy in Germany.

Migration and asylum: Germany has seen an influx of migrants and refugees in recent years, which has resulted in legal and policy debates over the country's obligations to protect the rights of asylum seekers and refugees.

Climate change: Germany has been at the forefront of efforts to combat climate change, and the country's legal system is playing an increasingly important role in this effort. For example, the country's highest court has ruled that the government must take more decisive action to reduce greenhouse gas emissions.

Hate speech and hate crimes: Germany has strict laws against hate speech and hate crimes, which are offenses motivated by prejudice or bias against a particular group, such as racial or ethnic minorities, LGBT individuals, or religious groups.

Labor and employment law: Germany has a complex legal framework that governs labor and employment relationships, including laws on working hours, wages, and job security.

Consumer protection: Germany has laws and regulations that protect the rights of consumers, including laws on product safety, advertising, and consumer credit.

These are just a few of the many important legal issues in Germany. The legal landscape in the country is constantly evolving, and new issues are constantly arising, reflecting the country's changing social, political, and economic landscape

In Germany, the law applies equally to all individuals, regardless of their background or immigration status. This means that refugees and immigrants can be held accountable for crimes they commit, just like any other individual. Additionally, the country has a criminal justice system that is designed to investigate and prosecute criminal offenses, regardless of who committed them. If a refugee or immigrant commits a crime in Germany, they can be subject to the same legal penalties as a native-born German. The law in Germany is designed to protect all individuals and communities, and it does not discriminate based on immigration status or other factors.

Chapter 19. The biggest challenges to German law in the future.

Technology and innovation: The rapid pace of technological advancement is creating new challenges for the legal system in Germany and around the world. As new technologies emerge, laws and regulations must keep pace in order to ensure that they are used in a way that is consistent with fundamental rights and values.

Globalization and cross-border legal issues: As the world becomes more interconnected, German law must increasingly deal with cross-border legal issues, such as the recognition and enforcement of foreign judgments, international contracts, and cross-border disputes.

Climate change: Climate change is a global challenge that will have far-reaching impacts on the legal system in Germany and around the world. Legal measures, such as emissions trading systems and carbon taxes, will be needed to address the effects of climate change, and the legal system must be prepared to adapt to the changing realities of this issue.

Migration and asylum: The ongoing refugee crisis and the resulting influx of migrants and refugees into Germany and other European countries is presenting significant legal and policy challenges. The legal system must ensure that the rights of refugees and migrants are respected and protected, while also balancing the needs of national security and public safety.

Data protection and privacy: The rapid growth of digital technologies and the increasing amount of personal data being generated and stored are presenting significant challenges to the protection of privacy and data rights. The legal system must continue to evolve in order to keep pace with these changes and ensure that privacy rights are respected.

These are just a few of the many challenges facing the legal system in Germany in the future. As the country and the world continue to evolve, the legal system will need to adapt in order to meet the changing needs and expectations of society.

Chapter 20. Prominent law cases in Germany.

The Berlin Wall Case: This was a landmark case in Germany in which the country's highest court ruled that the construction of the Berlin Wall was illegal.

The Federal Constitutional Court Case: This case concerned the power of the German government to impose measures to combat the spread of the COVID-19 pandemic.

The Adolf Eichmann Trial: This was the trial of former Nazi official Adolf Eichmann for war crimes committed during the Holocaust.

The Frankfurt Auschwitz Trials: These trials were held in Frankfurt in 1963 and 1965 and resulted in the conviction of 22 former Nazi officials for crimes committed during the Holocaust.

The TÜV Rheinland Case: This was a landmark case in which the German Federal Court of Justice ruled that the certification of a number of diesel vehicles by TÜV Rheinland was illegal.

The NSU Trials: This was the trial of the National Socialist Underground, a far-right terrorist group responsible for a series of murders and other crimes in Germany.

The Niemoeller Case: This was a landmark case in which the German Federal Court of Justice ruled that the imprisonment of Protestant pastor Martin Niemoeller during the Nazi regime was illegal.

Chapter 21. The training of lawyers in Germany.

In Germany, the training of lawyers typically consists of the following steps:

A university degree: To become a lawyer in Germany, one must first complete a university degree in law. This typically takes about six years.

The First State Exam: After completing a law degree, one must take and pass the First State Exam, which tests knowledge of legal theory and practice.

Legal clerkship: The next step is a two-year legal clerkship, also known as the "Referendariat," during which the trainee works in various legal fields, including the judiciary, law firms, and government agencies.

The Second State Exam: Upon completion of the legal clerkship, one must take and pass the Second State Exam, which tests practical legal skills and knowledge.

Admission to the bar: After passing the Second State Exam, one must be admitted to the bar, which is the professional association of lawyers in Germany. This requires passing a bar examination and meeting ethical standards set by the bar.

Once admitted to the bar, a lawyer can practice law in Germany and represent clients in court. Additionally, some lawyers may choose to specialize in a particular area of law, such as corporate law or criminal law, through additional training and education.

Chapter 22. The most broken laws in Germany.

Traffic violations: This includes speeding, running red lights, and not wearing seat belts.

Theft and burglary: This includes shoplifting, pickpocketing, and residential burglaries.

Drug offenses: This includes the possession, sale, and distribution of illegal drugs.

Fraud: This includes financial fraud, identity theft, and other forms of white-collar crime.

Assault and battery: This include physical assaults, sexual assaults, and domestic violence.

Environmental crimes: This includes illegal dumping of waste, air pollution, and water pollution.

Tax evasion: This involves not paying the correct amount of taxes owed to the government.

It's worth noting that the laws that are most frequently broken can vary depending on the location, time, and other factors. These are just a few of the most commonly reported crimes in Germany.

Chapter 23. A list of some common German legal terms:

Gesetz - Law

Vertrag - Contract

Recht - Right

Gericht - Court

Strafgesetzbuch - Criminal Code

Bürgerliches Gesetzbuch - Civil Code

Arbeitsrecht - Labor Law

Urheberrecht - Copyright Law

Markenrecht - Trademark Law

Patentrecht - Patent Law

Wettbewerbsrecht - Competition Law

Verwaltungsrecht - Administrative Law

Zivilprozessrecht - Civil Procedure Law

Strafprozessrecht - Criminal Procedure Law

Europäisches Recht - European Law

This is not an exhaustive list, but it should give you an idea of some of the key legal terms in the German language.

Chapter 24. How do you make a Vertrag (contract) in Germany?

Here are the general steps to make a contract (Vertrag) in Germany:

Determine the parties involved: The first step is to identify the parties who will be involved in the contract. This can include individuals, companies, or other entities.

Define the terms and conditions: The next step is to clearly define the terms and conditions of the contract, including the rights and obligations of each party. This should be done in writing and should be as specific and detailed as possible.

Sign the contract: Once the terms and conditions have been agreed upon, the contract should be signed by all parties involved. It is recommended to keep a copy of the signed contract for future reference.

Register the contract: Depending on the type of contract and the parties involved, it may be necessary to register the contract with a government agency or other official entity.

Comply with the terms and conditions: Once the contract is signed and registered, it is binding on all parties and should be followed in accordance with its terms and conditions.

It's important to note that contracts in Germany must comply with applicable laws and regulations, and that it's advisable to consult with a qualified legal professional to ensure that the contract is legally binding and enforceable.

Chapter 25. What is meant by Recht in German?

The German word "Recht" can have several meanings, including:

Law: Recht refers to the legal system and the body of laws that govern a society.

Right: Recht can also mean "right", as in a legal right or entitlement.

Justice: In a more abstract sense, Recht can refer to the concept of justice or fairness.

Overall, the meaning of "Recht" can vary depending on the context in which it is used. It is important to consider the context in which the word is used to determine its meaning accurately.

Chapter 26. Does everybody have a Recht?

In a democratic society, it is generally believed that everyone has certain inherent rights, such as the right to life, liberty, and property. These rights are often codified in a constitution or bill of rights and are protected by law.

However, the extent to which individuals have rights and the specific rights that they have can vary depending on the country and its legal system. In some countries, certain groups of people may not have the same rights and protections as others, and human rights abuses can occur.

Therefore, while the idea that everyone has rights is a fundamental principle in many societies, the reality is that the protection and enforcement of these rights can vary greatly.

Chapter 27. The balance between individual rights and freedoms and the interests of society.

In Germany, the balance between individual rights and freedoms and the interests of society is an important aspect of the legal system. The German constitution, known as the Basic Law, lays down the fundamental rights and freedoms of individuals, including freedom of speech, religion, and assembly, as well as the right to privacy and property. At the same time, the constitution also recognizes that these individual rights and freedoms must be balanced with the interests of society, such as the protection of public safety, the protection of the environment, and the protection of the rights of others.

The balance between individual rights and freedoms and the interests of society is maintained through a number of mechanisms, including the interpretation of laws by the courts, the role of the legislative branch in passing laws and regulations, and the role of the executive branch in enforcing laws and regulations. In some cases, the constitution itself provides guidance on how to balance these conflicting interests, for example, by requiring that any restriction on individual rights and freedoms be proportionate to the aims pursued.

The German legal system is designed to ensure that the rights and freedoms of individuals are protected, while at the same time ensuring that society is protected from harm. This balance is reflected in the laws and regulations that are passed by the legislative branch, and the way in which these laws are enforced by the executive branch and interpreted by the judiciary. Ultimately, the goal of the German legal system is to ensure that individual rights and freedoms are respected, while at the same time ensuring that society as a whole is protected and that the common good is served.

Chapter 28. Do foreigners have more rights in Germany than native Germans?

All individuals in Germany, regardless of their nationality, are entitled to the same basic rights and protections under the law. This includes the right to life, liberty, and security of a person, freedom of speech and religion, and protection from discrimination, among others.

However, non-citizens may have additional obligations and restrictions compared to citizens, such as the requirement to have a valid residency permit and to comply with immigration laws.

It is important to note that everyone in Germany, regardless of their nationality, is equal before the law and that all individuals have the right to access the legal system and to seek protection of their rights. Any discrimination on the basis of nationality, ethnicity, religion, or other grounds is prohibited by law.

Chapter 29. When do you have to go to the Gericht (court)?

A person may need to go to court (Gericht) in Germany for various reasons, including:

Civil disputes: When two or more parties have a dispute over a civil matter, such as a contract, property, or personal injury, they may need to go to court to have the dispute resolved.

Criminal proceedings: If a person is accused of committing a crime, they may need to go to court for criminal proceedings.

Family law: Family law issues, such as divorce, child custody, and child support, may require a person to go to court.

Administrative disputes: If a person is challenging a government decision or regulation, they may need to go to court to have the matter resolved.

It's important to note that going to court is usually a last resort and that many disputes can be resolved through alternative dispute resolution methods, such as mediation or arbitration. Additionally, it's advisable to consult with a qualified legal professional before going to court to ensure that you understand your rights and obligations, and to help navigate the legal process.

Chapter 30. Is the Strafgesetzbuch based on the laws of Napoleon?

The German Criminal Code (Strafgesetzbuch, or StGB) is not based directly on the laws of Napoleon, but its development was influenced by the Napoleonic Code.

The Napoleonic Code, also known as the French Civil Code, was enacted in 1804 and became a model for modern legal systems around the world. Its influence can be seen in the development of criminal law codes in many countries, including Germany.

The first draft of the German Criminal Code was written in the mid-19th century and was based on the principles of the Napoleonic Code. It was enacted in 1871 and has been amended several times since then. Today, the German Criminal Code remains one of the key sources of criminal law in Germany and continues to be influential in the development of criminal law codes around the world.

Chapter 31. The Strafgesetzbuch.

The Strafgesetzbuch (StGB) is the German Criminal Code, which is the primary source of criminal law in Germany. The StGB sets out the offenses that are considered criminal in Germany and the punishments that can be imposed for those offenses.

The StGB covers a wide range of criminal offenses, including violent crimes, property crimes, white-collar crimes, and offenses against public order. It also sets out the procedures that must be followed in criminal proceedings and the rights of the accused.

One of the key features of the StGB is its codification of the principle of legality, which means that criminal offenses and punishments must be clearly defined by law and cannot be arbitrarily imposed. This principle helps to ensure that the criminal justice system is fair and transparent.

The StGB is an important document in Germany and has a significant impact on the lives of individuals and society as a whole. It is constantly being reviewed and updated to reflect changes in society and to ensure that the criminal justice system remains fair and effective.

Chapter 32. The Bürgerliches Gesetzbuch.

The Bürgerliches Gesetzbuch (BGB) is the German Civil Code. It is the primary source of civil law in Germany and sets out the rules and regulations that govern private legal relationships between individuals and companies.

The BGB covers a wide range of civil law topics, including contract law, property law, family law, inheritance law, and consumer protection. It also sets out the procedures that must be followed in civil proceedings and the rights of the parties involved.

One of the key features of the BGB is its codification of the principle of good faith, which requires individuals and companies to act fairly and honestly in their dealings with one another. This principle helps to ensure that legal relationships are based on trust and cooperation.

The BGB is an important document in Germany and has a significant impact on the lives of individuals and businesses. It is constantly being reviewed and updated to reflect changes in society and to ensure that civil law remains fair and effective.

Chapter 33. The Bürgerliches Gesetzbuch, a short history.

The Bürgerliches Gesetzbuch (BGB) was enacted in Germany on January 1, 1900. Its development was part of a larger movement to modernize and unify German civil law, which was previously fragmented and based on various regional laws.

The process of creating the BGB began in the mid-19th century and involved a team of legal experts and scholars who worked together to draft a comprehensive and unified civil code for the entire country. The final draft of the BGB was based on several sources, including the Napoleonic Code, which was the model for many modern legal systems at the time, as well as German legal traditions and practices.

The BGB was enacted into law as part of the process of unifying and modernizing German law following the country's unification in 1871. It has been amended several times since then to reflect changes in society and to ensure that civil law remains fair and effective.

Today, the BGB remains one of the key sources of civil law in Germany and continues to play an important role in shaping the legal landscape and protecting the rights of individuals and businesses.

Chapter 34. Arbeitsrecht - Labour Law

Arbeitsrecht is the German law that governs the relationship between employers and employees. It covers all aspects of employment, from the hiring process, to the terms and conditions of employment, to the termination of employment.

Arbeitsrecht sets out the minimum rights and obligations of employees and employers, and it provides a framework for the resolution of disputes that may arise between them. For example, the law sets out minimum notice periods for termination of employment, and it provides for the right of employees to bring claims for unfair dismissal or discrimination.

The law also regulates the working hours and conditions of employment, such as overtime, breaks, and holiday entitlements. It also sets out rules on health and safety in the workplace, and it provides for the right of employees to join trade unions.

Overall, Arbeitsrecht is an important aspect of the German legal system, as it helps to ensure that employees are treated fairly and with dignity, and it provides a means for resolving disputes between employers and employees.

Chapter 35. Urheberrecht - Copyright Law

Urheberrecht is the German copyright law. It protects the rights of creators of original works, such as literary, artistic, and musical works, as well as software and databases. Urheberrecht gives the creators of these works the exclusive right to control how their works are used and exploited, including the right to make copies, distribute, and display their works.

The law also provides for the protection of moral rights, which are the personal rights of the creator to be recognized as the author of their works and to object to any changes that would damage their reputation.

Urheberrecht is an important aspect of the German legal system, as it provides a framework for the protection of intellectual property and helps to ensure that creators are fairly compensated for their work. The law also helps to foster creativity and innovation by providing incentives for people to create and produce original works.

Overall, Urheberrecht plays a crucial role in ensuring that creators are able to control the use and exploitation of their works and that they are fairly compensated for their contributions to society.

Chapter 36. The German Markenrecht - Trademark Law

The German Markenrecht is the trademark law in Germany. It provides protection for trademarks and service marks, which are distinctive signs used to identify and distinguish goods or services from those of other traders.

Markenrecht gives the owner of a trademark the exclusive right to use that trademark in connection with the goods or services for which it is registered. This includes the right to prevent others from using the same or similar trademark in a way that is likely to cause confusion among consumers.

The law also provides for the registration of trademarks, which gives the owner a legal right to use the trademark and to enforce their rights against others. The registration process involves a review of the trademark by the German Patent and Trademark Office, which ensures that the trademark is distinctive and not confusingly similar to other existing trademarks.

Markenrecht is an important aspect of the German legal system, as it helps to protect the rights of trademark owners and ensures that consumers are not confused or misled by the use of similar trademarks. The law also helps to promote fair competition and to foster innovation and creativity by providing legal protection for distinctive signs that are used to identify goods and services.

Overall, Markenrecht plays a crucial role in promoting the interests of trademark owners, consumers, and the wider business community in Germany.

Chapter 37. Patentrecht - Patent Law

Patentrecht is the German patent law. It provides protection for inventions and allows inventors to exclude others from using, selling, or manufacturing their inventions without their permission.

Patentrecht gives inventors the exclusive right to exploit their inventions for a certain period of time, usually 20 years from the date of filing. During this time, no one else may make, use, sell or import the invention without the inventor's permission.

The law also provides for the examination and grant of patents, which involves a review of the invention by the German Patent and Trade Mark Office (DPMA) to ensure that it is new, inventive, and industrially applicable. Once granted, a patent provides a legal right for the inventor to enforce their rights against others who may use the invention without their permission.

Patentrecht is an important aspect of the German legal system, as it provides protection for inventions and encourages innovation and creativity by giving inventors the right to exploit their inventions. The law also promotes fair competition and protects the public by ensuring that inventions are disclosed and can be freely used after the term of the patent has expired.

Overall, Patentrecht plays a crucial role in fostering innovation, promoting fair competition, and protecting the interests of inventors and the public in Germany.

Chapter 38. Wettbewerbsrecht - Competition Law

Wettbewerbsrecht is the German competition law. It aims to promote fair competition and prevent anti-competitive practices, such as price fixing, abuse of a dominant market position, and anti-competitive agreements.

Wettbewerbsrecht sets out rules on anti-competitive practices and provides for the enforcement of these rules by government agencies, such as the Federal Cartel Office. The law also provides for the right of private individuals and businesses to bring claims for damages caused by anti-competitive practices.

The law also regulates the merger and acquisition of companies to ensure that these transactions do not lead to the creation of dominant market positions or anti-competitive practices. The Federal Cartel Office carries out investigations into proposed mergers and acquisitions to ensure that they comply with the competition laws.

Wettbewerbsrecht is an important aspect of the German legal system, as it helps to promote fair competition and prevent anti-competitive practices. The law also protects the interests of consumers by ensuring that they are not exposed to artificially high prices or limited choices due to anti-competitive practices.

Overall, Wettbewerbsrecht plays a crucial role in ensuring that the market operates in a fair and competitive manner, and it helps to protect the interests of consumers, businesses, and the wider economy in Germany.

Chapter 39. Verwaltungsrecht - Administrative Law

Verwaltungsrecht is the German administrative law. It governs the relationships between citizens and the state and sets out the rights and obligations of citizens and the responsibilities of the state.

Verwaltungsrecht governs the actions of administrative bodies, such as government agencies and departments, and regulates the powers and duties of these bodies. It sets out the procedures that administrative bodies must follow when making decisions, including the right of citizens to be heard and to challenge decisions.

The law also provides for judicial review of administrative actions, which means that citizens can seek a court review of decisions made by administrative bodies. This helps to ensure that administrative actions are consistent with the law and that citizens are protected against arbitrary or unreasonable actions by the state.

Verwaltungsrecht is an important aspect of the German legal system, as it provides a framework for the relationship between citizens and the state and helps to ensure that administrative actions are consistent with the law and with the rights and obligations of citizens. The law also helps to promote transparency and accountability in the actions of administrative bodies.

Overall, Verwaltungsrecht plays a crucial role in ensuring that the state operates in a fair, transparent and accountable manner, and that the rights and interests of citizens are protected.

Chapter 40. Zivilprozessrecht - Civil Procedure Law

Zivilprozessrecht is the German civil procedure law. It sets out the rules and procedures for conducting civil lawsuits in the German courts.

Zivilprozessrecht provides for the initiation, conduct and resolution of civil proceedings, including the rights and obligations of parties, the rules of evidence, and the standards for decision making. The law also governs the powers and duties of the courts, including the power to issue injunctions, to award damages, and to enforce court decisions.

The law also provides for alternative dispute resolution mechanisms, such as mediation and arbitration, which allow parties to resolve disputes without going to court. These mechanisms are designed to provide a quicker and less formal resolution of disputes and to avoid the costs and delays associated with traditional litigation.

Zivilprozessrecht is an important aspect of the German legal system, as it provides a framework for resolving civil disputes and helps to ensure that civil proceedings are conducted in a fair and efficient manner. The law also promotes access to justice and provides a means for individuals and businesses to enforce their rights and to seek remedy for wrongs.

Overall, Zivilprozessrecht plays a crucial role in ensuring that civil disputes are resolved in a fair, efficient and accessible manner, and it helps to promote the rule of law and to protect the rights and interests of citizens and businesses in Germany.

Chapter 41. Strafprozessrecht - Criminal Procedure Law

Strafprozessrecht is the German criminal procedure law. It sets out the rules and procedures for conducting criminal trials in the German courts.

Strafprozessrecht governs the rights and obligations of the accused, the prosecution, and the courts in criminal proceedings. The law provides for the right to a fair trial, the right to counsel, and the right to remain silent. It also sets out the rules of evidence, the standards for decision-making, and the procedures for appeal.

The law also provides for the powers and duties of the police, the prosecution, and the courts in investigating and prosecuting criminal cases. It regulates the use of evidence, the rights of the accused to challenge evidence and to cross-examine witnesses, and the standards for decision-making.

Strafprozessrecht is an important aspect of the German legal system, as it provides a framework for conducting criminal trials and helps to ensure that the rights and interests of the accused, the prosecution, and the public are protected. The law also promotes transparency and accountability in the administration of justice and helps to ensure that criminal cases are resolved in a fair and impartial manner.

Overall, Strafprozessrecht plays a crucial role in ensuring that criminal trials are conducted in a fair, transparent and accountable manner, and it helps to promote the rule of law and to protect the rights and interests of citizens in Germany.

Chapter 42. Europäisches Recht - European Law

Europäisches Recht is the European law, which governs the relationships between the European Union (EU) and its member states, and between the EU and its citizens.

European law consists of a complex system of laws and regulations that apply to all EU member states and their citizens. It includes the EU treaties, which establish the framework for the EU, and the EU legislation, which consists of regulations, directives and decisions that are binding on all member states.

European law takes precedence over national law in situations where there is a conflict between the two. This means that national courts must apply European law in cases where it is relevant and where it conflicts with national law.

European law is an important aspect of the EU legal system, as it helps to ensure that the EU operates in a consistent and harmonious manner and that the rights and interests of citizens are protected. The law also promotes cooperation between member states, helps to eliminate barriers to trade and commerce, and helps to ensure that the EU operates in a transparent and accountable manner.

Overall, Europäisches Recht plays a crucial role in shaping the relationships between the EU and its member states and between the EU and its citizens, and it helps to promote cooperation, transparency and accountability in the operation of the EU.

Chapter 43. The relationship between EU Law and German Law.

The relationship between EU law and German law is complex and dynamic, with EU law having a significant impact on the legal system in Germany. EU law takes precedence over national law in all member states, including Germany, meaning that if there is a conflict between EU law and national law, EU law must be applied.

In Germany, EU law is incorporated into the legal system through a number of mechanisms, including the principle of direct effect, which allows individuals to rely on EU law in national courts, and the principle of supremacy, which means that EU law takes precedence over national law. The German Constitutional Court also plays an important role in interpreting EU law and ensuring that it is in compliance with the German constitution.

The relationship between EU law and German law is constantly evolving, as new EU legislation is adopted and new cases are decided by the European Court of Justice (ECJ). The ECJ is the highest court in the EU and is responsible for interpreting and applying EU law, and its decisions have a binding effect on all EU member states, including Germany.

In addition to the direct impact of EU law on German law, the relationship between the two is also influenced by the German legal system's commitment to the rule of law and the protection of individual rights and freedoms. This commitment is reflected in the way in which EU law is interpreted and applied in Germany, with the German courts taking a rigorous approach to ensuring that EU law complies with the principles of the German constitution.

In conclusion, the relationship between EU law and German law is complex and dynamic, with EU law having a significant impact on the legal system in Germany. Through mechanisms such as the principle of direct effect and the role of the German Constitutional Court, the German legal system has ensured that EU law is incorporated into the legal system in a way that respects the rule of law and protects individual rights and freedoms

Conclusion

In conclusion, the German legal system is a complex and sophisticated system that has played a significant role in shaping not only the legal landscape of Germany, but also influencing the development of legal systems around the world. From its roots in Roman law and the development of the German Civil Code in the 19th century, German law has evolved over time to meet the changing needs of society, while still retaining its fundamental principles of fairness, justice, and the protection of individual rights and freedoms.

Throughout this book, we have explored the key components of the German legal system, including the role of the judiciary, the interaction between different branches of government, and the balance between individual rights and freedoms and the interests of society. By examining these components, we have gained a deeper understanding of the German legal system and its place in the world today.

As the German legal system continues to evolve and adapt to new challenges and opportunities, it is important to remember the rich history and fundamental principles that have shaped it into the world-class legal system that it is today. Whether you are a student of law, a practitioner, or simply someone with an interest in legal systems, this book has provided a comprehensive and accessible introduction to the world of German law, and we hope that it has helped you to understand the intricacies of the German legal system and appreciate its significance both within Germany and on the global stage.

Printed in Great Britain
by Amazon